RUBANK EDUCATIONAL LIBRARY No. 145

Concert and Contest COLLECTION

for

C FLUTE

with piano accompaniment

Compiled and Edited
by H. VOXMAN

Contents

Gavotte

Flute
FR. JOS. GOSSEC
Edited by H. Voxman
Allegretto
p
p
mf
rit
a tempo
Fine
f
f
mf
p
p
cresc.
f
D. C. al Fine

Bergamask

Flute

PAUL KOEPKE
Edited by H. Voxman

Serenade

Flute

VICTOR HERBERT, Op. 3
Edited by H. Voxman

Scherzino

Flute

JOACHIM ANDERSEN, Op. 55, No. 6
Edited by H. Voxman

mf liberamente
p lesto
cresc.
f
p
mobile
mf
p
rfz
p
mf
p mobile
mf
p
mf
f
mf
dim.

p
pp
pp
1

Valse Gracieuse

Flute

W. POPP, Op. 261, No. 2
Edited by H. Voxman

94
mf
p scherzando

103

110
cresc.

117
2
mf
f

129
a tempo
p
rit.
p

139
mf
p

148

154
1
p

160
1
mf
mf

168
f
f

174
ff

Andalouse

Flute

ÉMILE PESSARD, Op. 20
Edited by H. Voxman

Flute

cresc.
f
a tempo di più mosso
rit.
ff
rit.
a tempo I
p
p
f
Più lento
rit.
dolce
ten.
ritard.
a tempo
ten.
rit.
ten.
a tempo
rit.
7
7
più p
perdendo e rit. molto
pp

Menuet
from
L'Arlésienne Suite No. 2

Flute

GEORGES BIZET
Edited by H. Voxman

Flute

sempre f
sempre f
sempre f
sempre f
pp espress.
pp
cresc.
sf
dim.
pp
pp
calando e smor - zand - o
(long)
ppp

Serenade

Flute

JOS. HAYDN
Edited by H. Voxman

Siciliana and Giga

from

Sonata V

Menuet and Spirit Dance

from Orpheus

Flute

C. W. von GLUCK
Edited by H. Voxman

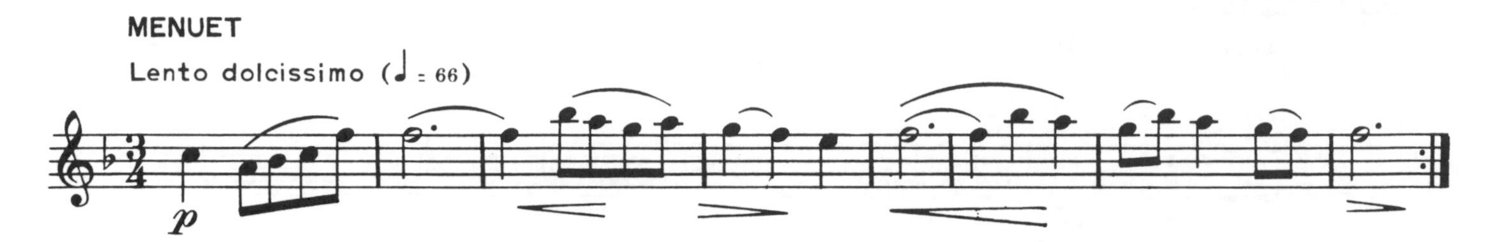

46
p
cresc.

50
f
p subito
f

54
dim.
p
cresc.

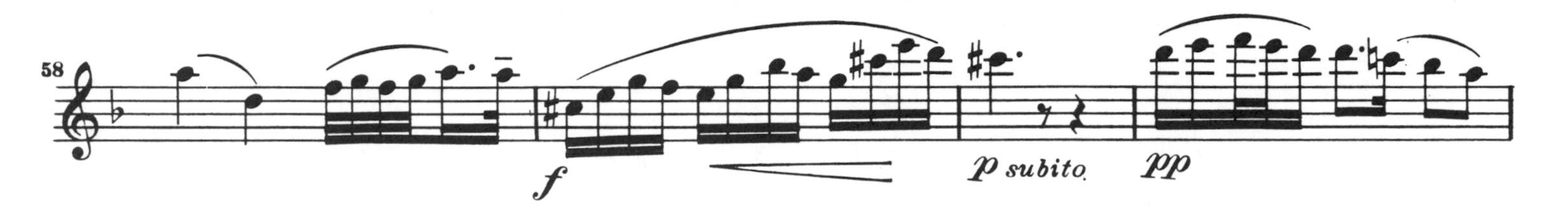
58
f
p subito
pp

62
tr
riten.
fz

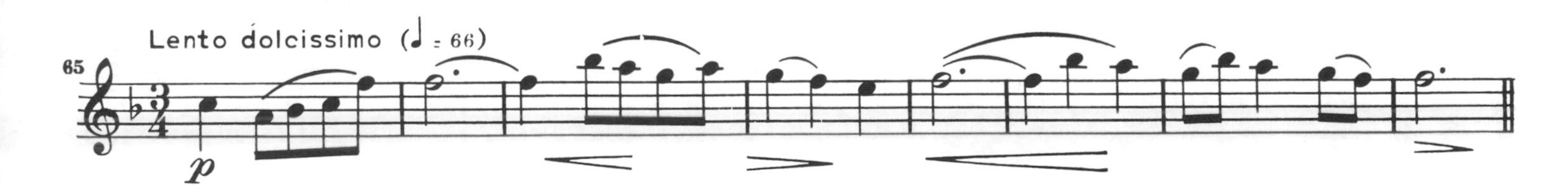
Lento dolcissimo (♩ = 66)
65
p

73
pp
p
cresc.
f

84
p

Polonaise and Badinerie

from

Suite in B Minor

Flute

J. S. BACH

Edited by H. Voxman

Flute
BADINERIE
Presto
cresc.

Romance

Flute
GEORGES BRUN, Op. 41
Edited by H. Voxman
Modéré, sans lenteur
(Moderately, without dragging)
mf
Calme
Un peu retenu (a little slower)
Un peu animé
(a little faster)
f
Toujours animé (always animated)
mf Chaleureux (with warmth)
pp cre - - scen - - do
Tempo
rallent.
Plus calme
(more quietly)
rallent.
Plus lent
(More slowly)
mf très expressif et chanté
(very expressively and in a singing style)
Copyright MCMXLI by Rubank, Inc., Chicago, Ill.
International Copyright Secured

cre - - scen - do
(with animation)
Animez
1er Mouvt plus vite que le 12/8
(Tempo I, faster than 12/8)
rallent.

Un peu retenu
Tempo
Sans lenteur, avec un peu d'animation

Un peu ralenti

Tempo
Calme
Lent

22
Flight of the Bumblebee
from
The Legend of the Czar Sultan
Flute
N. RIMSKY-KORSAKOFF
Edited by H. Voxman
Vivace (♩ = 144)
Piano
sf
dim.
p
optional
optional
optional
optional
p

Flute

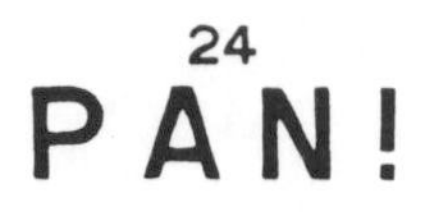

PAN!

Flute

Pastorale

J. DONJON
Edited by H. Voxman